Endorsements for *Tracing Oracle*

"I use trace data, because putting all the technical terminology aside
for a moment, if you've got a list of everything that happened, when
it happened, and how long it took to happen, then much of the task
of understanding is complete. And trace data gives you exactly that."

—Connor McDonald, developer advocate at Oracle, and
one of the mentors behind *asktom.oracle.com*

"I use extended SQL trace for identifying bottlenecks
because that is the most efficient and extensive way to
perform a controlled measurement while an application is
experiencing a reproducible performance problem."

—Christian Antognini, author of
Troubleshooting Oracle Performance

"When you trace an application, you are basically asking it
to describe what it is doing so that you can help improve its
performance. You can learn so much just by asking."

—Guðmundur Jósepsson, director and
performance specialist at Inaris

"If you want to start understanding why Oracle performs
the way it does, you need to start using SQL trace."

—Toon Koppelaars, author of *Applied
Mathematics for Database Professionals*

"Trace files show us what's happening behind the scenes, early
in our development process where we can fix problems long
before they could ever affect anyone using our products."

—Andrew Zitelli, aerospace software engineer
and IndyCar race enthusiast

The ◇ METHOD R Guide to

TRACING
ORACLE

The ◇ Method R *Guide to*

TRACING
ORACLE

Cary Millsap
Jeff Holt

◇ Method R™

◇ MᴇᴛHᴏᴅ Rᵀᴹ

Method R Corporation, Southlake, Texas 76092

https://method-r.com

© 2023 Cary Millsap

Published 2023

Revised May 11, 2023 2:34 PM

28 27 26 25 24 23   1 2 3 4 5

ISBN-13: 979-8370854668 (paperback)

Editor, compositor, indexer, cover designer: Cary Millsap

Copy editors, proofreaders, and technical reviewers: Guðmundur Jósepsson, Nancy Spafford, Richard Soule, Martin Berger.

For everyone who wants to see
how your Oracle system spends your time.

I've become convinced that all compilers written from now on should be designed to provide all programmers with feedback indicating what parts of their programs are costing the most.

—Donald E. Knuth

Contents

V   Scoping ₂₁

VI   Levels ₂₉

VII   Specific Technologies ₃₅

Preface

Tracing is a superpower. It's X-ray vision for computer programs. And it's the only way you can answer all four of the most important questions about performance:

1. *How long* did that user's experience take (this click, that report, …)?

2. *Why?* How did the experience spend its time?

3. *What if* we change something? How will the experience's duration react?

4. *What else* can we do? Can we further improve the experience? Or have we reached the limit of what's possible?

But lots of Oracle DBAs and developers don't trace. It's usually because:

- They don't know how.

- They're afraid.

- The tools for working with Oracle traces aren't very good.

If this describes you, it's not your fault. Oracle teaches ASH and AWR, not tracing, so naturally, tracing is going to feel more alien to you. Whenever Oracle does mention tracing, they warn you to expect degraded performance, so it's no wonder people are afraid. And, yes, the tools that Oracle gives you for working with trace files are no fun to use.

We wrote this book to help you through all of these problems. You'll learn how to trace (we'll step you through it). You'll conquer your fear of tracing (we'll show you how to do it safely). And you'll meet some sophisticated tools you can buy to do amazing work with traces, even if you create thousands of them (we'll introduce you).

If you're one of those DBAs or developers who hasn't traced in a while, chances are excellent that some of your programs are running less efficiently than they should be—or maybe even less *correctly*. When you master tracing, you'll see problems that you wouldn't have found any other way.

Cary Millsap

Acknowledgments

Thank you to the following people who have helped us create this book:

Darrell Abbott, Ali Abdul Hakeem, Nick Achin, Martin Berger, Venkata Bhetanabhotla, Mathew Butler, Gianni Ceresa, Clement Chan, Dallas Deeds, Pete Dinin, Paul Ellingwood, Steven Feuerstein, Marc Fielding, David Frankel, Doug Gault, Dimitri Gielis, Brian Hill, Sriram "Sri-Bob" Iyer, Lasse Jenssen, Gummi Jósepsson, Andy Klock, Sayan Malakshinov, Jackie McIlroy, Anton Nielsen, Jimmy Payne, Krzysztof Przepiórka, Richard Soule, Nancy Spafford, Jared Still, Lars Johan Ulveseth, Chandramouli Venkatasubramanian.

And thank you to the following people for their generosity and inspiration:

Steve Adams, Chris Antognini, Jorge Barba, Dimas Chbane, Mark Clark, Maria Colgan, Ron Crisco, Dominic Delmolino, Johannes Djernæs, Julian Dontcheff, Dave Ensor, Eric Evans, Mark Farnham, Ken Ferlita, Monty Free, Alex Gorbachev, Stephan Haisley, Tim Hall, Frits Hoogland, Anjo Kolk, Toon Koppelaars, Steven Kotler, Tom Kyte, Jonathan Lewis, Connor McDonald, Brendan McNamee, James Morle, Karen Morton, Mogens Nørgaard, Kerry Osborne, Harold Palacio, Rafael Pereira, Tanel Põder, Jorge Rimblas, Andy Rivenes, Christoph Ruepprich, Virag Saksena, Abdul Sheikh, Edward Tufte, Mark Williams, Graham Wood, Steve Wyper, Winston Zhang, Andrew Zitelli.

Tracing Oracle at GitHub

Many of the operations described in this book are available as open source programs at *https://github.com/CaryMillsap/tracing-oracle*. Just about everywhere you see a reference to a table name or something that sounds like it should be a script, have a look at our repository. We might have already written what you need.

There are package definitions in the repository that we especially hope you'll study. One package is for developers (MRDEV), and the other is for database administrators (MRDBA). They demonstrate one way of providing safe and convenient access to the tracing facilities described in this book.

Not every software tool mentioned in this book is distributed free at GitHub. Applications like Dynatrace (*https://www.dynatrace.com*) and Method R Workbench (*https://method-r.com*) are commercially licensed software products sold by their respective owners and distributors.

Oracle Database Versions

This book was written and tested using the following Oracle Database versions:

- *Oracle DB Developer VM (macOS)*
  Oracle Database 19*c* Enterprise Edition, Version 19.3.0.0.0

- *Oracle DB Developer VM (macOS)*
  Oracle Database 23*c* Free—Developer Release, Version 23.2.0.0.0

- *ADB-S (Oracle Autonomous Database on shared infrastructure)*
  Oracle Database 19*c* Enterprise Edition, Version 19.19.0.1.0

- *ADB-D (Oracle Autonomous Database on dedicated infrastructure)*
  Oracle Database 19*c* EE Extreme Perf, Version 19.18.0.1.0

I Getting Started

1 Hello, World

If you've never traced Oracle before, let's get that out of the way right now.

If you're the commander of your own Oracle instance,[1] then you can execute the following script in an interactive query tool like SQL Developer, SQLcl, or SQL*Plus. The script will trace the experience of a simple SELECT and then show you the name of your trace file:

```
1. connect system
2. exec dbms_monitor.session_trace_enable
3. select 'hello, world' from dual;
4. exec dbms_monitor.session_trace_disable
5. select value from v$diag_info where name='Default Trace File';
```

If you're using someone else's system, then you'll need someone who can connect as SYS to grant you one privilege before you can use DBMS_MONITOR:

```
1. grant execute on dbms_monitor to dev1;
```

On a real system, your DBA may not want to grant you this privilege. We describe a more production-friendly permission strategy in chapter 4.

---

1. Any Oracle Database except an Oracle Autonomous Database on shared infrastructure (ADB-S). If you're using ADB-S, then please jump to page 59.

2 What Is a Trace?

An Oracle *trace* is a stream of data written by an *Oracle kernel process* (your *server process*) that lists information such as:

- the name of a database call (dbcall), like "PARSE", "EXEC", or "FETCH"
- the name of a system call (syscall), like "db file scattered read"
- the duration of the call
- the time at which the call ended
- the identity of the SQL or PL/SQL statement that motivated the call
- the execution plan for each query executed
- the values bound into SQL or PL/SQL statement placeholders

You can manipulate the trace feature by calling various stored procedures.[2] Different trace *levels* dictate how much information is included in a trace.

Oracle tracing is historically referred to as *event 10046 tracing*, because it is listed in $ORACLE_HOME/rdbms/mesg/oraus.msg as Oracle "pseudo-error debugging event" number 10046. In version 6 (1988), Oracle had a SQL trace feature that showed timings for dbcalls only. In version 7 (1992), Oracle began showing timings for syscalls as well, and the enhancement took the name *extended SQL trace*.

Today, all editions of Oracle Database offer the extended SQL trace feature except for ADB-S, which offers only the version 6–era SQL trace feature.[3]

---

2.   ...Or by using ALTER statements, which we do not recommend (chapter 41).

3.   See page xvii for Oracle Database versions that were current at this book's publication time.

3   Why Trace?

Why trace? Because a trace reveals information you can't get any other way. Only with a trace can you explain unambiguously why a user's experience consumes the time that it does. A trace is the only way to answer the four most important questions you can ask about performance:

1. Exactly *how long* does that user's experience with the application take?

2. *Why* does the experience consume the time that it does?

3. *What if* you were to implement one remedy attempt or another? How exactly would it change the experience duration?

4. *What else?* Is further improvement for that experience even possible?

Maybe a more important question is, why do people *not* trace? Here are the reasons we most often encounter:

- They don't realize how much tracing would help them.

- They're afraid that tracing will make their performance problems even worse.

- They're overwhelmed by the amount of data that tracing creates.

- They're not satisfied with the results of using Oracle tools like `tkprof`.

- They're taught to rely on other technologies like ASH and AWR.

- They want to trace, but they're not granted the privileges required to do it.

- They think tracing should be someone *else*'s responsibility.

It's been our mission since 1999 to overcome the obstacles that stop developers and DBAs from tracing. The first step is learning how to trace properly. That's what this book is all about. The second step is to acquire the knowledge and the tools to extract all the stories that your traces are trying to tell you. That's what our much bigger book, *The Method R Guide to Mastering Oracle Trace Data*,[4] and our Method R software products[5] (part XI) are all about.

---

4. *https://method-r.com/motd.*

5. *https://method-r.com/#software.*

II Preliminaries

4   Privileges

We believe that DBAs should be able to trace any program in any environment. Endowed with the normal DBA role, they can do that:[6]

```
1.  grant dba to dba1;   -- for database administrators
```

We also believe that application developers should make *tracing* an application feature that users can use to make their software more observable in any environment, including production. Developers should be able to write code that enables and disables tracing, accesses their traces, and sets their Oracle user session handle attributes.

Oracle doesn't make tracing for developers as easy as it could have been. It's easy to fix though. You can create a custom package to provide access to all the tracing facilities that a developer needs. In fact, we've done it for you. Our MRDEV package at *GitHub* puts a convenient and secure wrapper around all the trace-related procedures a developer will need access to.

---

6.   ADB-S doesn't work this way. For information about ADB-S tracing, jump to page 59.

5 Parameters

Before you trace, you need to confirm that the following Oracle parameters are set to trace-friendly values, at least for the sessions you want to trace; better yet, for your whole system:

DIAGNOSTIC_DEST=*dir*

> Setting DIAGNOSTIC_DEST=*dir* causes Oracle to write trace files to *dir*/diag/
> rdbms/*db-unique-name*/*oracle-sid*/trace. The default value of DIAGNOSTIC_
> DEST is derived from the value of the ORACLE_BASE environment variable if
> ORACLE_BASE is set, or from the value of ORACLE_HOME if ORACLE_BASE is not
> set. Make sure that the filesystem containing your DIAGNOSTIC_DEST directory
> has enough size (bytes) capacity and throughput (IOPS) capacity to handle
> the writing of however much data your traces will generate (chapter 37).

MAX_DUMP_FILE_SIZE=UNLIMITED

> Set MAX_DUMP_FILE_SIZE=UNLIMITED (the default on many systems) so that
> the Oracle kernel will not restrict the size of your trace file. Your team *will*
> need to ensure that your trace files don't fill your DIAGNOSTIC_DEST filesystem
> (chapter 7), but restricting MAX_DUMP_FILE_SIZE is not the best way to do that
> (chapter 6).

STATISTICS_LEVEL=TYPICAL

> Set STATISTICS_LEVEL=TYPICAL (the default) unless you have a special need
> to use STATISTICS_LEVEL=ALL (which may add significant measurement
> intrusion effect to your traces). Don't use STATISTICS_LEVEL=BASIC, which
> prevents your Oracle kernel from measuring time, which renders tracing
> mostly useless.

6   MAX_DUMP_FILE_SIZE

There's a problem with restricting MAX_DUMP_FILE_SIZE.

Imagine this: a user has been suffering every month over a ridiculously long-running program. But you've got a new book and a new plan. You'll trace the user's experience. This program doesn't run every day, just once a month, so you've been preparing for weeks to catch this thing in the act of being slow. Today's the day you're going to do it. Today, you'll *finally* learn what the problem is.

So the user runs the program. You can see its trace file. It's growing, …yes, the trace is working! And then, about 30 seconds into the program's expected 2-hour-long execution, the file stops growing. That's weird. The program's still running, but the trace is frozen. At exactly 10 MB.

You open the trace file, and the last line says this:

```
*** DUMP FILE SIZE IS LIMITED TO 10485760 BYTES ***
```

Unfortunately, that's all the trace data you'll be getting from this program—about half a minute's worth—until next month.[7]

Always use MAX_DUMP_FILE_SIZE=UNLIMITED when you trace. We know you're worried about your DIAGNOSTIC_DEST filesystem filling up (chapter 7). But you're probably going to regret it if you try to manage your space consumption by limiting MAX_DUMP_FILE_SIZE.

---

7.   The Oracle Database product does have a helpful-sounding feature called *trace file segmentation*, which *might* give you some of the information you're hoping to find. But unless you write a complicated program to retain all the data that Oracle writes into its trace file segments—*in real time*—trace file segmentation is not going to be of near as much use to you as if you just set MAX_DUMP_FILE_SIZE=UNLIMITED like we're suggesting.

7 Trace File Hygiene

Tracing writes to the same filesystem where your alert log is stored. If that filesystem fills, then any attempt to write to the alert log will cause an outage. So you'll need a trace file retention policy. Here are some ideas about that:

- Don't ever delete a trace file that's being held open by a running process.[8]

- If the only trace files you're interested in have already been copied someplace else for analysis (like an analyst's workstation), then you probably don't need to retain your trace files on your server for more than a day or two.

- If there are people outside your group who create and use trace files, then you'll need to find out their retention requirements.

- If you need a long retention period, consider using gzip to compress files, and consider moving your older traces to another filesystem.

- If there's nothing really complicated going on (and if there is, then your team has probably already addressed it), then you'll probably be fine running a nightly command to delete .trc and .trm files that are more than N days old, where N is something like 7, 14, or 28. Our *GitHub* repository has an example.

- You probably already have an alert that will signal your system administrators when a filesystem comes close to running out of space. For the first week or two of new tracing activity, your team may need to adjust their thresholds to accommodate the new activity.

After your first few experiences with tracing, the whole team will have a good idea about how much extra space you're going to have to worry about managing. For most people, the files end up not consuming nearly as much space as they had feared.

---

8. When an Oracle kernel process receives an error trying to write to a file that you've deleted, it won't hurt the process; it will simply open a new trace file. However, the process will not re-write any PARSING IN CURSOR information into the new file that it had already written into the old file. Thus, the new file won't contain the information you'll need to identify which SQL statements account for the work that's taking place.

8   Be Kind, Please Rewind

If your DBA or sysadmin team have carefully set a system parameter to something other than the Oracle Database default value, then the polite thing to do when you change its value is to set it back the way you found it when you're done tracing.

If you're tracing only your own session, then it's easy: just alter your session, trace your program, and then disconnect from Oracle. But if you've used an ALTER SYSTEM command to change a system parameter's value, then the polite thing to do is set it back when you're done.

Either that, or negotiate that your parameter's value going forward should be the Oracle Database default.

III Tracing

9   How to Trace a SQL Script

If you're an application developer who wants to measure a sequence of SQL or
PL/SQL statements , then you need to make sure there's no time lapse between
the steps of enabling your trace, running your statements, and disabling the trace.
The best way to make sure of that is to put the enable/run/disable steps all in the
same SQL Developer or SQLcl script together, like this:[9]

```
1.  @trace-on              -- Enable tracing
2.  @YOUR-PROGRAM.sql      -- Your program runs here
3.  @trace-off             -- Disable tracing
4.  @my-trace-file         -- Show the trace file name
5.  exit                   -- Let Oracle close the trace file.
```

Don't let *any* extra time lapse between the enable, run, and disable steps.
Otherwise, you'll end up needing to do extra work to fix a *scoping error*
(chapter 16).

---

9. We have a script in *GitHub* that does this.

10 How to Trace Someone Else's Session

Oracle's DBMS_MONITOR gives you the ability to enable and disable traces in someone *else's* session, like this:

```
 1.  -- Example: trace session whose Oracle session ID is 1492.
 2.  exec dbms_monitor.session_trace_enable(1492)
 3.  /* Wait for session 1492 to complete the activity you want traced. */
 4.  exec dbms_monitor.session_trace_disable(1492)
 5.
 6.  -- Example: create a standing order to trace a user's executions.
 7.  exec dbms_monitor.client_id_trace_enable('NGRIF')
 8.  /* All client_id='NGRIF' programs will be traced. */
 9.  exec dbms_monitor.client_id_trace_disable('NGRIF')
10.
11.  -- Example: create a standing order to trace a module's executions.
12.  exec dbms_monitor.serv_mod_act_trace_enable('APPS1','PAYROLL')
13.  /* All programs whose (service,module) = ('APPS1','PAYROLL') will be traced. */
14.  exec dbms_monitor.serv_mod_act_trace_disable('APPS1','PAYROLL')
15.
16.  -- Example: trace an entire database
17.  exec dbms_monitor.database_trace_enable
18.  /* All database programs will be traced. */
19.  exec dbms_monitor.database_trace_disable
```

These "standing order" procedures are great for tracing that 2:00 a.m. batch job whose name you know. You can simply instruct the system to trace programs that identify themselves a certain way, and the database will take care of tracing them for you automatically when they run.

11 How to Clean Up Your Enabled Traces

Creating standing orders with DBMS_MONITOR is tremendously helpful, but you need to be able to clean up after yourself. You don't want to leave a bunch of standing orders enabled that will start traces you neither want nor need. You can see what traces you've enabled by selecting from DBA_ENABLED_TRACES.[10] Then you can use the appropriate DBMS_MONITOR...DISABLE procedure to disable the trace directives you no longer need.

---

10. Of course, we have a script in *GitHub* for that.

IV Access

12 Trace Directory Names

A client program can see its trace file directory name by querying V$DIAG_INFO. A DBA can find someone else's trace file directory name by querying V$PROCESS.

Oracle writes trace files into the following directory on your database server:

> *dir*/diag/rdbms/*db-unique-name*/*oracle-sid*/trace/

…where

- *dir* is the DIAGOSTIC_DEST Oracle parameter value,
- *db-unique-name* is the database site-wide name, and
- *oracle-sid* is the database instance name.

On a multi-node Oracle RAC system, your files may be distributed across two or more servers, each with the same *db-unique-name* but a different *oracle-sid*.

13 Trace File Names

Users can access their own sessions' trace file names by querying V$DIAG_INFO. A DBA can find someone else's trace file name by querying V$PROCESS. Trace file names look like this:

oracle-sid_pname_spid.trc

...where

- *oracle-sid* is the database instance name,
- *pname* is a process name (ora for a typical server process), and
- *spid* is the Oracle kernel process's OS process ID.

There are lots of process names you might see.[11] Here are just a few:

pname	Process
ora	Oracle Server
arc*n*	Oracle Archiver
dbw*n*	Oracle Database Writer
lgwr	Oracle Log Writer
mmon	Oracle Manageability Monitor
pmon	Oracle Process Monitor
j*nnn*	Oracle Scheduler
s*nnn*	Oracle Shared Server
d*nnn*	Oracle Dispatcher
p*nnn*	Oracle Parallel Execution (PX) child

If a session has set its TRACEFILE_IDENTIFIER attribute,[12] then its trace file name will contain an extra string at the tail of the file's base name. For example, if you set TRACEFILE_IDENTIFIER='test42', then your trace file name will look like prod_ora_1492_**test42**.trc.

---

11. *Dyke, "Trace File Names."*

12. ...Which we advise against (chapter 40).

14 Accessing Your Trace without Filesystem Access

A client program can query its own trace data from V$DIAG_TRACE_FILE_ CONTENTS. Well, *most* of its own trace data. The PAYLOAD column has a VARCHAR2(4000) data type, so a line longer than 4,000 characters risks truncation or bugs.[13]

You can access *all* of your trace data with SQL using a database DIRECTORY object.[14] There are programs written in both Java and Perl to do it at our *GitHub* repository.

---

13. For example, Oracle bug 31528203.

14. Holt: "Fetching Oracle trace data."

15 Identifying Your Trace Files

When you have several different `DBMS_MONITOR` calls enabled at the same time, how can you tell which files belong with each experience? You'll be able to identify each trace file by observing the "✱✱✱" lines near the top of the file:

```
1. *** 2022-06-20T16:35:30.120273-04:00 (ablt(3))
2. *** SESSION ID:(3015.27846) 2022-06-20T16:35:30.120309-04:00
3. *** CLIENT ID:(CMINTON) 2022-06-20T16:35:30.120315-04:00
4. *** SERVICE NAME:(ebs_ablt) 2022-06-20T16:35:30.120321-04:00
5. *** MODULE NAME:(e:INV:cp:inv/INCFDH) 2022-06-20T16:35:30.120326-04:00
6. *** ACTION NAME:(INV/INVENTORY_USER) 2022-06-20T16:35:30.120331-04:00
7. *** CLIENT DRIVER:() 2022-06-20T16:35:30.120336-04:00
8. *** CONTAINER ID:(3) 2022-06-20T16:35:30.120341-04:00
```

The value for each user session handle attribute (client ID, service, module, and action) is reported in parentheses.

V   Scoping

16 What Is Scoping?

We trace because we want to learn the answers to questions like, "Exactly how did my program spend the 18 minutes that I waited for it to complete?" To answer a question like that, you need trace data that explains precisely what happened to *that specific program execution* (that's the *task scope*) during *that specific time interval* (that's the *time scope*).

Ideally, you want a report formatted like a grocery store receipt explaining where every microsecond of that 18 minutes has gone. Indeed, a trace that is properly scoped in both the *task* and *time* dimensions can be summarized into such a receipt-like format (chapter 52).

In contrast, here's what you *don't* want, because it doesn't answer your real question about your 18-minute experience:

- You *don't* want data that explains what resources all the programs on your system consumed during your 18-minute experience. That's bad task scoping.

- You *don't* want data that explains everything your user did during a one-hour interval that contains part or even all of the 18-minute experience. That's bad time scoping.

- And you certainly don't want data that explains what resources all the users on your system consumed over a one-hour interval. That's bad scoping in *both* dimensions.[15]

It's tempting to just collect the data that's easiest to collect. But you need the data that best helps you answer your real questions, even if it's harder to collect.

> *The goal of tracing is to match the time and task scope of your trace to the time and task scope of the experience you're wanting to diagnose.*

So, choose carefully both *when* to trace and *what* to trace.

---

15. This is approximately what an Oracle AWR report gives you. ...Except in sampled form (that is, with data missing), and with potentially critical data (so-called "idle" waits) discarded.

17 How Should *You* Trace?

There are lots of ways to trace. Which one should you choose? Here's our answer, ranked in precedence order. We try to stay as close to the top of the list as we can:

1. If the experience of interest is a script, then execute your script like we show in chapter 9.

2. If the application sets a distinct client ID for each experience, then use DBMS_MONITOR.CLIENT_ID_TRACE_ENABLE.

3. If the application sets a distinct module and action name for each experience, then use DBMS_MONITOR.SERV_MOD_ACT_TRACE_ENABLE.

4. If the program runs long enough that someone can identify its session ID before too much of its execution duration has passed, then use DBMS_MONITOR.SESSION_TRACE_ENABLE.

5. If your problem is a single SQL statement with a known SQL_ID, then trace by SQL_ID with DBMS_USERDIAG.ENABLE_SQL_TRACE_EVENT.[16]

6. If the experience of interest has specific actions at the beginning and end (for example, inserting into a log table) then create triggers on these actions to use DBMS_MONITOR.SESSION_TRACE_ENABLE and ...DISABLE.

7. If there is some *x* for which SYS_CONTEXT('USERENV', *x*) identifies the program executions that you want to trace, then trace the program executions you want with an AFTER LOGON trigger.

8. If you can create a new trace-enabled service or connection pool to which users can connect whenever they want to trace, then use DBMS_MONITOR.SERV_MOD_ACT_TRACE_ENABLE.

9. Otherwise, use DBMS_MONITOR.DATABASE_TRACE_ENABLE. Don't summarily refuse a DATABASE_TRACE_ENABLE. It may be at the bottom of our list, but it's *on* our list for good reason. We've solved problems with database-wide traces that we'd never have solved any other way.

---

16. DBMS_USERDIAG is a package introduced in Oracle Database 23c. Prior to 23c, the only way to trace by SQL_ID is by using ORADEBUG (chapter 41), which we hesitate to recommend.

18 How Application Developers Can Make Tracing Easier

Our favorite way to trace a user experience is when the developer of the application has been thoughtful enough to use DBMS_SESSION.SET_IDENTIFIER to set a program execution's client ID value, and DBMS_APPLICATION_INFO.SET_MODULE to set a program execution's module and action values.[17]

If a developer has been thoughtful enough to set an application's Oracle user session handle attributes to identifying values that DBAs can hook using DBMS_MONITOR.SERV_MOD_ACT_TRACE_ENABLE and DBMS_MONITOR.CLIENT_ID_TRACE_ENABLE, then tracing is easy!

Now a developer can tell a DBA, over coffee, "Hey, our order clerks have a big stress test tomorrow on DEV02 of some new features my group has written. Would you please trace all executions of our Book Order feature in tomorrow's 10:00–11:00 a.m. window? Here are the details…"

```
trace enable 10:00 a.m.
trace disable 11:00 a.m.
instance 'DEV02'
module 'OE'
action 'Book Order'
```

---

17. Yes, it's weird that you can't set your program's client identifier with DBMS_APPLICATION_INFO like all the other session handle attributes, but you can't. The procedure to set your client identifier is in DBMS_SESSION. We take care of this problem in our MRDEV package definition at *GitHub*.

19 trcsess

trcsess is an Oracle command-line utility that consolidates data from one or more trace files. It's a scoping tool. When you call trcsess upon a list of trace files, you'll specify one or more of the following constraints:[18]

```
session=session_id
service=service_name
module=module_name
action=action_name
clientid=client_id[19]
```

trcsess will find the chunks of trace data that matches all of your constraints and then concatenate those chunks chronologically into its output. This is useful whenever one session writes trace data into two or more files:[20]

```
trcsess session=294.31072 output=294.trc *.trc
```

...Or when two or more sessions write trace data into one file:[21]

```
trcsess session=294.31072 output=294.trc x_ora_123.trc
```

Unfortunately, trcsess leaves important information out of its output. For example, if you run "trcsess session=294.31072 *.trc", you might expect to see lines like these (from your input) in your output:

```
Trace file /u01/app/oracle/diag/rdbms/x/x/trace/x_ora_123.trc
*** SESSION ID:(294.31072) 2023-04-12T16:26:59.533401+00:00
```

But the trcsess output will contain only this instead:

```
*** 2023-04-12T16:26:59.533401+00:00
```

This behavior is frustrating. It makes double-checking trcsess much more difficult than it needed to be, and it forces you do extra work to keep your files organized.

---

18. Oracle, "Performing Application Tracing."

19. This is not a typo: the client ID option name (clientid) has id at the end. None of the other option names end in name or id.

20. Oracle shared server sessions do this, as do sessions that set TRACEFILE_IDENTIFIER (chapter 40).

21. Shared server sessions do this as well, as do sessions in a connection pool (chapter 29).

20 APPINFO

SQL Developer, SQLcl, and SQL*Plus all use DBMS_APPLICATION_INFO.SET_
MODULE to set your session's MODULE attribute. The APPINFO system variable,[22]
which you can SHOW and SET, controls the behavior:

	MODULE	
Client	APPINFO OFF	APPINFO ON
SQL Developer	SQL Developer	*nn filename*
SQLcl	SQLcl	*nn filename*
SQL*Plus	SQL*Plus	*nn@ filename*

...where

- *nn* is the nesting level of the script being executed (for example, a script called from a top-level 01 script will have level 02), and
- *filename* is the name of the script being executed.

This feature helps Oracle's command line interface utilities cooperate with
DBMS_MONITOR.SERV_MOD_ACT_TRACE_ENABLE[23] and any tool that groups by user
session handle attributes. If you want to set your session's ACTION or CLIENTID
values, you'll need to do it yourself with DBMS_APPLICATION_INFO and DBMS_
SESSION.

---

22. Oracle calls it a "system variable," but it's really an environment setting for your current session.

23. But wouldn't it be nice if SERV_MOD_ACT_TRACE_ENABLE did a regular expression match instead of a simple string equality match?

21 Tracing with Triggers

What can you do when the code you want to trace doesn't set its session handle attributes, and it executes so quickly that you don't have time to identify its Oracle session ID? You can use a trigger. It's one of the wonders of the Oracle world that you can actually interject *your* code path into another person's code path—even in a sealed third-party application.

We'll use, for example, an AFTER LOGON trigger to execute DBMS_MONITOR. SESSION_TRACE_ENABLE for a user with a specific name. You could extend that concept to enable tracing if the user's name is listed in a table that you've created. Triggers, coupled with the information available from, for example, the SYS_ CONTEXT SQL function, give you enormous flexibility.

You can also trigger on DML statements that mark experience boundaries. For example, an experience that begins with "INSERT INTO MY_LOG" and ends with the first subsequent "UPDATE MY_LOG" is a candidate for the following triggers, using DBMS_MONITOR:

- In a "BEFORE INSERT OF MY_LOG" trigger, call SESSION_TRACE_ENABLE.

- In an "AFTER UPDATE OF MY_LOG" trigger, call SESSION_TRACE_DISABLE.

22 Tracing a Whole Database

Intermittent problems can be particularly bothersome; for example, how do you diagnose a system that executes 100,000 transactions every hour, and only ten of them time out? You never know in advance which transactions—or even which *kinds* of transactions—will end badly, so how can you choose which ones to trace?

The answer is the same as how they catch shoplifters: you film *everybody*.

That's right, you trace the entire database. The first questions we always get is, "But won't that slow everything down even worse?"

The answer is, no, tracing won't slow anything down, *if you do it right*. We have customers who've done it, in production, for hours at a time. But they were careful how they did it. They chose the right level (chapter 24). They wrote their traces to a high-performance storage array (chapter 37). They tested and measured, using tools like Dynatrace,[24] to confirm that response times with tracing enabled were indistinguishable from response times with tracing disabled (chapter 39). And they had an escape plan for disabling their traces immediately if a problem—or even a perceived problem—arose (chapter 36).

The second question we get is, "What are we going to do with all that data?" The answer is that you need tools that can handle hundreds or even thousands of trace files, like Method R Workbench (chapter 52).

---

24. *https://www.dynatrace.com/*.

VI Levels

23 Trace Levels

When you trace a session, you get to decide what *level* to use. In the old days, the levels were numbers, like 0, 1, 4, 8, 12, 28, and 44. Modern tracing interfaces let us use names instead of numbers. Names are better. Here are the names that you get to use in the DBMS_MONITOR and DBMS_USERDIAG PL/SQL packages:

WAITS

> The WAITS option controls tracing of syscalls.
>
> – WAITS=>TRUE (the default) enables syscall tracing.
>
> – WAITS=>FALSE suppresses syscall tracing.

BINDS

> The BINDS option controls tracing of the operations that bind values to placeholders (like the ":b1" in "select name from t where id=:b1").
>
> – BINDS=>TRUE enables binds tracing.
>
> – BINDS=>FALSE (the default) suppresses binds tracing.

PLAN_STAT

> The PLAN_STAT option controls tracing of execution plans.
>
> – PLAN_STAT=>'NEVER' disables execution plan tracing.
>
> – PLAN_STAT=>'FIRST_EXECUTION' (the default) prints a plan into the trace only after the last row of the first execution is processed.
>
> – PLAN_STAT=>'ALL_EXECUTIONS' prints a plan into the trace after the last row of each execution is processed.
>
> – PLAN_STAT=>'ADAPTIVE' prints a plan into the trace once for every minute of dbcall time consumed per cursor.[25]

---

25. DBMS_MONITOR doesn't recognize the value PLAN_STAT=>'ADAPTIVE' in Oracle Database versions prior to 23.

24 Which Level Should You Use?

Which trace level should you use? Use the default values until you have proven (by testing) that it's OK to do otherwise:

```
WAITS=>TRUE
BINDS=>FALSE
PLAN_STAT=>'FIRST_EXECUTION'
```

25 Why We Recommend Not Tracing BINDS

Knowing what values are being bound into SQL *placeholders* (also known as *bind variables*) is vital to diagnosing some problem types. In the early 2000s, we used to always recommend tracing bind operations. But one day, using BINDS=>TRUE nearly tripled the duration of a program we were tracing. It turned out that our program had made a gazillion EXEC calls upon a SQL statement with hundreds of placeholders.

Here's why that matters: every time an application binds a value to a placeholder, a BINDS=>TRUE trace causes Oracle to write 5 lines (about 180 bytes) into the trace file, using *two* write calls per line.[26] So, an EXEC that might consume only a few hundred microseconds when BINDS=>FALSE has to write an extra 36 KB to the trace file with 2,000 extra write calls when BINDS=>TRUE:

$$200 \text{ placeholders} \times 180 \text{ bytes/placeholder} = 36{,}000 \text{ bytes}$$
$$200 \text{ placeholders} \times 5 \text{ lines/placeholder} \times 2 \text{ writes/line} = 2{,}000 \text{ writes}$$

That's an outrageous amount of extra work for an EXEC to have to do. When the program you're tracing is written to process just one row at a time,[27] executing gazillions of short-duration EXEC calls, it intensifies the effect.

We never want you to get burned by tracing, so we recommend using BINDS=>FALSE until you know you don't have any SQL statements with lots of placeholders and high EXEC call frequencies. If you do have such SQL statements, then you'll see them with a BINDS=>FALSE trace. Once you've proven, using BINDS=>FALSE, that a program doesn't have this kind of a problem, then it's OK to trace it with BINDS=>TRUE.

---

26. One write call for the content, and another for the line terminator. It's just how Oracle works.

27. *Kyte, "Slow by Slow..."*

26 Why We Recommend Not Tracing ALL_EXECUTIONS

When you trace execution plans with the PLAN_STAT option, Oracle writes about 150 bytes to the trace for every row source operation in the plan. Certainly, it's almost always important for a trace to contain an execution plan. Sometimes a single execution of the same statement might use different plans, and when that happens, of course you want to know it.

But it's common for a customer to send us a trace file with statements whose execution plans have 500-plus 150-byte row source operations in them. Can you imagine how much longer it would take each EXEC call to finish if Oracle had to write 75,000 = 500 × 150 extra bytes with 1,000 = 500 × 2 extra write calls to the trace *every time that statement is executed?*[28]

This is why we recommend using PLAN_STAT=>'FIRST_EXECUTION' or PLAN_STAT=>'ADAPTIVE', at least until you know that your application doesn't have huge execution plans for statements with high execution frequencies. Only then is it safe to use PLAN_STAT=>'ALL_EXECUTIONS'.

---

28. The "× 2" in the write call count calculation is because Oracle uses two separate write calls for each line (chapter 25).

VII Specific Technologies

27 Oracle APEX

To trace an Oracle Application Express (APEX) page, append &p_trace=YES to its URL.[29] This will create a file in your DIAGNOSTIC_DEST directory, called:

*oracle-sid*_ora_*spid*_f-*sessid*-*time*.trc

…where

- *oracle-sid* is the database instance name,
- *spid* is the OS process ID of the Oracle server process that writes the trace,
- *sessid* is the APEX session ID listed in the APEX page URL,[30] and
- *time* is a timestamp computed when the file is opened.

Tracing an APEX page with &p_trace=YES creates a WAITS=>TRUE, BINDS=>TRUE, PLAN_STAT=>'FIRST_EXECUTION' trace. The BINDS=>TRUE part is contrary to our usual advice, but APEX offers no way to manipulate the trace level. Fortunately, an APEX form is not likely to exhibit the problems described in chapter 25 and chapter 26.

If you are an APEX workspace administrator, you can start a trace of another user's session by clicking the *Administration* icon and choosing *Monitor Activity* › *Active Sessions* › *Session Detail* › *Trace Mode = SQL Trace*. You can also manipulate an APEX session's *Trace Mode* using PL/SQL:

```
1.  -- Example: trace the session whose APEX session ID is 1492.
2.  exec apex_session.set_trace(p_session_id=>1492, p_mode=>'SQL')
3.  commit;
4.  /* Execute the APEX experience (e.g., page, dynamic action, region) to trace. */
5.  exec apex_session.set_trace(p_session_id=>1492, p_mode=>null)
6.  commit;
```

---

29. For &p_trace=YES to work, *Manage Instance* › *Feature Configuration* › *Monitoring* › *Enable Application Tracing* must be set to its default value of *Yes*.

30. You can also find your APEX session ID by clicking *Session* in the APEX Developer toolbar.

28 Oracle E-Business Suite

You can trace Oracle E-Business Suite (EBS) sessions like any other application, but there are some features built into the product to make tracing a little easier. My Oracle Support Doc ID 1674024.1[31] lists detailed steps for tracing Forms programs, HTML/Self-Service (OAF) programs, and Concurrent Manager programs. It's an excellent document, and the instructions are sound. Just keep in mind the following:

- Choose *SQL Trace with Waits* (LEVEL 8) unless you know that its safe to choose *SQL Trace with Binds and Waits* (LEVEL 12) (chapter 25).

- Don't use TRACEFILE_IDENTIFIER unless you're willing to accept the cost of doing so (chapter 40).

- Use DBMS_MONITOR.SESSION_TRACE_ENABLE instead of an ALTER SESSION command (chapter 41).

---

31. *Oracle: "SQL Trace and TKPROF Guide"*

29 Oracle Connection Pooling

Connection pooling reduces Oracle connection management overhead by configuring application programs to share connections. When you use a connection pool, a single Oracle session can serve many different user experiences.

If your application's developers have been thoughtful enough to write programs that set their MODULE, ACTION, and CLIENT_IDENTIFIER user session handle attributes to well-chosen values, then DBMS_MONITOR gives you exactly the targeting you need for well-scoped connection pool tracing (with CLIENT_ID_TRACE_ENABLE and SERV_MOD_ACT_TRACE_ENABLE). But if your application's developers didn't set their programs' session handle attributes to well-chosen values, then your tracing options (listed in chapter 17) are limited.

If you trace a whole service or a whole database, your trace files will contain a mishmash of potentially thousands of user experiences. You can pick out relevant spans from your traces either manually, or with good tools. Method R Workbench is the only commercial tool we know that helps you extract user experience data from connection pool trace files (chapter 52).

Ideas for identifying interesting spans from connection pool trace data include:

- Isolating periods of activity amidst spans of inactivity: our *oceans–islands–rivers* algorithm.[32]

- Identifying periods of activity devoted to specific input values revealed by using BINDS=>TRUE.

---

32. *Millsap, "Oceans, Islands, Rivers."*

30 Oracle Parallel Execution

We use traces to diagnose programs that use Oracle's declarative parallel execution (PX) feature as well as single-threaded ones. Happily, when you trace a program, its tracing attribute is inherited by any PX children your program happens to fork.

But unfortunately, there's no way to tell from the trace file names or from information in any of the V$ or GV$ fixed views which PX worker trace files are associated with which PX coordinator. The only way to know which PX trace files "go together" is by examining the time stamps and sqlid values within your trace files.

If you use RAC, then be aware that your PX children trace files may be distributed across RAC nodes.

31 Oracle Scheduler

When you schedule a job with Oracle Scheduler, `DBMS_SCHEDULER` sets the job's user session handle attributes like a good application should. It sets the job's module name to "`DBMS_SCHEDULER`" and its action name to the value of its `JOB_NAME` attribute. This praiseworthy behavior makes Oracle Scheduler jobs easy to trace with `DBMS_MONITOR.SERV_MOD_ACT_TRACE_ENABLE`.

32 Oracle Cloud Infrastructure

The catalog of Oracle Cloud Infrastructure (OCI) services is itself so elastic that it wouldn't be practical to try to discuss each of those services or their tracing idiosyncrasies here. But you can characterize the traceability of any given service by two attributes: the ability to *control* tracing (that is, the power to start and stop tracing when you want, at the level you want), and the ability to *access* the traces you create.

To control tracing, you'll need EXECUTE privileges on DBMS_MONITOR. And to access your traces, you'll need at least one of the following:

- Direct filesystem access to the trace directory
- CREATE DIRECTORY privilege
- Access to some file replacement technology, like the Oracle Object Store
- A trace view, like V$DIAG_TRACE_FILE_CONTENTS or SESSION_CLOUD_TRACE

Traceability on OCI is a spectrum. Some services make tracing easy; for example, DBaaS, IaaS, ExaCS, and ExaCC give you full DBA and filesystem access. But other services (such as those based on ADB-S) restrict or even prohibit tracing entirely.

We know that self-managing databases are important. But so is observability. So we recommend that you factor traceability into your decision about what database services to buy (chapter 51). During your demo or test drive, ensure that your users will have access to the resources you need to endow your application with the observability you require. If you can't trace, then you're sacrificing a significant value.

33 Amazon RDS for Oracle

To trace an Amazon Relational Database Service (RDS) Oracle application, you'll use DBMS_MONITOR. But instead of accessing your trace files directly from the operating system, you'll access them through SQL. RDS provides a PL/SQL package called RDSADMIN.MANAGE_TRACEFILES, which lets you list trace file names and contents, set file retention durations, purge files, and so on.

However, the instructions at *aws.amazon.com* for spooling the content of a trace file[33] don't work for trace lines that are more than 400 characters long. To retrieve a high-fidelity copy of your actual trace, you can fetch the data through an Oracle DIRECTORY object (chapter 14).[34] Some Java and Perl code to do this are provided at our *GitHub* repository.

---

33. *Amazon: "Oracle database log files."*

34. *Holt: "Fetching Oracle trace data."*

34 Oracle Database 23c

Just before this book was published, Oracle released its Oracle Database 23c Free Developer Edition. There are two bits of good news to share.

First, DBMS_MONITOR still works, so all of the extraordinary tracing features we use with 10g through 19c also work in 23c. The presence of DBMS_MONITOR in 23c implies that Oracle intends to support our favorite tracing package into the foreseeable future.

Second, the 23c Free release has a new package called DBMS_USERDIAG that has some tracing features in it. Two of its procedures are especially interesting:

 - ENABLE_SQL_TRACE_EVENT gives you an alternative interface to some of the functions provided by DBMS_MONITOR.SESSION_TRACE_ENABLE. It also allows you to trace by SQL_ID, which previously you could do only with ORADEBUG (chapter 41).

 - CHECK_SQL_TRACE_EVENT makes it easy for a session to inquire about its own tracing status, without requiring V$SESSION access.

DBMS_USERDIAG is undocumented in the first 23c Developer Edition release, but you can see its definition by executing DESCRIBE SYS.DBMS_USERDIAG.

VIII Objections

35 Will Tracing Slow Everything Down?

The first thing people usually ask when we suggest a trace is, "How much of a performance penalty will it cause?" The performance penalty of tracing is *unnoticeable* if you do it right. That's important, because the last thing you want is for your diagnostic process to make your users' suffering even worse than it already is.

If you do it right, a program with tracing enabled will run within ±5% of the duration that it consumes with tracing disabled. Since most program durations fluctuate by more than 5% from run to run anyway, tracing—done properly— doesn't cause an effect that anybody using the application will notice.[35]

We encourage you to measure the effect for yourself. One of our Fortune 500 customers used Dynatrace[36] to confirm that *none* of their program execution durations were noticeably different with tracing enabled, even when they traced database-wide for several hours.

It's important to make sure that your traces are being written to fast storage. The main difference between tracing and not tracing is whether your kernel process writes its timing data to a file. Your V$ and X$ performance views require the same timer calls whether you're tracing or not.

---

35. It's not unusual for repeated executions of the same command to fluctuate 10% or more. You can see it happen even a simple command like "`time find . -print > x`".

36. *https://www.dynatrace.com.*

36 What If Tracing *Does* Slow Something Down?

We don't expect for tracing to slow anything down, but what if it does? Or what if somebody just mistakenly *thinks* that your trace is slowing something down? The middle of a crisis (either real or imagined) is no time to be inventing your rollback procedure. You need to have done that up front.

For tracing, your rollback procedure is simple: clean up your enabled traces, using DBMS_MONITOR (chapter 11). Have your trace-disable script ready at hand, so that you can disable tracing instantaneously upon becoming aware of the need to do so.

And consider this…

Maybe it's worth tracing a program even if it *does* slow that program down while you're tracing it.

Imagine a 30-minute program that runs 10 times a day. Imagine that tracing it causes one of its runs to take 15 extra minutes. That shouldn't happen, but maybe you've ignored our advice in chapter 25 or chapter 26. Finally, imagine that the trace would reveal how to improve the program's duration to 1 minute per run.

If you think of the trace as a 50% performance overhead, it sounds so punitive that might avoid doing it. But if you think of it as a one-time 15-minute investment that helps you reduce your users' collective misery by 290 minutes per day,[37] it becomes a value that shouldn't ignore.

---

37. 10 runs/day $\times$ $(30 - 1)$ minutes/run $= 290$ minutes/day.

37 Trace Rates and Sizes

Will tracing fill your filesystem? It's a question you'll need to answer, because if it does, for example, it will prohibit your Oracle Database instance from writing to its alert log file, which will appear to the business like an outage.

The best way to know how big a trace will be is to test it. Different programs can generate trace data at radically different rates, and testing is the best way to acquire a feel for how much space your files will consume.

Most of the trace files we've seen were generated at a rate of between 10 KB and 500 KB per second. The worst we've seen is a trace write rate of about 10 MB/s for one Oracle process. Trace files typically compress to about 10% of their original size.

If you want to try to predict your trace file sizes, here are the typical sizes of the basic elements:

Per traced...	Bytes	Writes
dbcall (PARSE, EXEC, FETCH, ...)	100	2
syscall (WAIT)	160	2
bind (BINDS)	180	10
row source operation (STAT)	150	2

Oracle writes a few other things to your trace in addition to these, like the text of each SQL statement your program parses while tracing is enabled. But the factor that dominates the size and rate of a WAITS=>TRUE, BINDS=>FALSE, PLAN_STAT=>'FIRST_EXECUTION' trace is generally its program's call velocity, which you can estimate by querying V$SYSSTAT.

If you really want to know how big your trace files will be, the answer is *testing*. You'll find the real answer by testing and measuring.

38 Data Security

A trace, which an Oracle process writes to a file, can contain
sensitive information:

- It can contain sensitive data in SQL code, like "UPDATE EMPLOYEE SET
  SALARY=1000000 WHERE SSN='078-05-1120'".[38]

- If you trace binds, then it can contain information bound into SQL
  statement placeholders. For example, if the statement above had
  said "…WHERE SALARY=:A1 AND SSN=:A2", then you'd see the strings
  "value=1000000" and "value='078-05-1120'" in the trace.

If a trace file does contain sensitive information, then you need to control who
has access to it. If you need to share a trace file with a diagnostician who doesn't
have clearance to see all of its contents, then you have the following options:

- Change your diagnostician. Either find a diagnostician with the right
  clearance, or improve the clearance of the one you have. A signed non-
  disclosure agreement may be all that you need.

- Change your trace file. Either write or buy a program to obfuscate a trace's
  sensitive data.

- Change how you trace. If a program can bind sensitive information to
  placeholders in your SQL text, then use BINDS=>FALSE.

- Change your application. Make sure that a program never embeds sensitive
  information directly into its SQL or PL/SQL text.

---

38. Code that looks like this should have never been written this way in the first place. Good SQL
    should use placeholders that have values bound into them at runtime. Code that embeds values
    in its text doesn't scale, because it requires too many PARSE dbcalls to run. Also, such code is
    prone to SQL injection security breaches.

39 Safeguards

Are you afraid to trace in production? It's fair to be afraid until you test it. A careful plan is your best defense against a mistake that could cause harm (or just embarrass) you. When you trace, especially in production, you need a plan that incorporates at least the following elements:

- Test your tracing strategy. It's important: *test your tracing strategy.* Testing will help you find Oracle tracing bugs (which are rare), problems with parameters like STATISTICS_LEVEL or MAX_DUMP_FILE_SIZE, and any surprises that may be unique to your system or situation.

- Trace at the right level. For example, don't trace binds if the application might make a lot of lightweight EXEC calls upon SQL with lots of placeholders. Don't trace plans for all executions if the application might make lots of lightweight EXEC calls for SQL statements with complex execution plans.

- Don't enable more traces than your storage array can handle. Make sure that both the size (bytes) capacity and throughput (IOPS) capacity of the storage devices you're tracing to are sufficient to handle the load.

- Make a plan for disabling traces *immediately* in case you encounter a situation in which—whether fairly or not—people might begin to perceive that a trace is hurting the business.

IX Proscriptions

40 Don't Use TRACEFILE_ IDENTIFIER

People use TRACEFILE_IDENTIFIER to make their trace files easier to find. It's a nice idea, but trace file names are easy enough to find already from V$DIAG_ INFO (chapter 1) or V$PROCESS (chapter 13). The problem with TRACEFILE_ IDENTIFIER is that it's too easy to lose data.[39] Here's why.

Setting TRACEFILE_IDENTIFIER=*string* causes a session that's tracing to close its existing trace file and open a new one with *string* in its name. So now there are *two* trace files associated with the session being traced:

```
prod_ora_1492.trc          # before "alter session set tracefile_identifier"
prod_ora_1492_test15.trc   # after "alter session set tracefile_identifer='test15'"
```

Oracle will write a helpful message in each file explaining the relationship:

At the end of prod_ora_1492.trc (the first file):
```
*** TRACE CONTINUES IN FILE /path/prod_ora_1492_test15.trc ***
```

Near the beginning of prod_ora_1492_test15.trc (the second file):
```
*** TRACE CONTINUED FROM FILE /path/prod_ora_1492.trc ***
```

That's fine, but sometimes Oracle writes PARSING IN CURSOR information into the first file that you can't see when you're analyzing the second file. So, here's what happens. Someone sends you a trace file with an identifier in its name. The file shows tons of activity but no statement text, so you have no idea what SQL or PL/SQL is causing your problem. The PARSING IN CURSOR sections you needed were in the first file that they didn't send—or keep.

Even if you're careful to retain both trace files, you may have to do extra work knitting them together to match the time and task scope of your user's experience. It's just easier not to use TRACEFILE_IDENTIFIER than it is to solve the problems it can cause. Use V$DIAG_INFO or V$PROCESS to identify your trace files. You'll be better off.

---

39. *My Oracle Support SR 3-32741539641.*

41 Don't Trace with ALTER Statements

If you were a DBA in the 1990s, you probably have this statement committed permanently to muscle memory:

```
alter session set events '10046 trace name context forever, level 8'
```

We recommend against DBAs using ALTER SESSION or ALTER SYSTEM syntax to control traces, because it's unnecessarily risky. If you mistype the level number, you can cause serious performance problems. If you mistype the event number, you can crash your instance. For example, event 10461 simulates a control file corruption. To control tracing, it's safer to use DBMS_MONITOR or DBMS_USERDIAG.

You probably don't want non-DBAs to have the ALTER SESSION system privilege to begin with. One reason is that ALTER SESSION is an interface to an internal Oracle library called ORADEBUG. This library (which is in fact invoked in the statement above) gives you access to some wild features including heap dumps, memory pokes, pool flushes, and the like.[40] You don't want people doing those kinds of things on a production system without strict Oracle supervision.

---

40. Põder, "ORADEBUG."

42 Don't Trace with the DBMS_SESSION Package

Oracle provides DBMS_SESSION.SESSION_TRACE_ENABLE and ...DISABLE procedures that *seem* like they'd be good for developers to use, but they're not. You can't use these procedures anywhere in your call stack unless you've been granted the ALTER SESSION system privilege. That's because (1) DBMS_SESSION. SESSION_TRACE_ENABLE uses an ALTER SESSION statement, and (2) DBMS_ SESSION is an invoker's rights package.

Since most developers won't have ALTER SESSION (nor should they),[41] most developers won't be able to use DBMS_SESSION.SESSION_TRACE_ENABLE (or any procedure that calls it). The only people who will be able to use it are DBAs, but DBAs don't *need* DBMS_**SESSION**.SESSION_TRACE_ENABLE, because they already have DBMS_**MONITOR**.SESSION_TRACE_ENABLE.

The bottom line? The DBMS_SESSION tracing procedures aren't much use to anybody. We recommend for you to ignore them. Just wrap procedures around DBMS_MONITOR for your developers to use, like we've done at *GitHub*.[42]

We're not recommending a ban on using DBMS_SESSION altogether. There's other good stuff in there that doesn't require ALTER SESSION, like the SET_IDENTIFIER procedure, which we definitely hope you'll use. But for controlling traces, stay away from DBMS_SESSION.

---

41. You don't want them having, for example, access to ORADEBUG (chapter 41).

42. DBMS_MONITOR is a well-mannered, definer's rights package whose procedures you can call securely from other procedures and functions.

43 Don't Trace with the SQL_TRACE Parameter

Some people grew up tracing like this:

```
1.  -- Bad example: don't do this.
2.  alter session set sql_trace=true;
3.  /* Wait for the session to complete the activity you want traced. */
4.  alter session set sql_trace=false;

5.  -- Bad example: don't do this.
6.  exec dbms_session.set_sql_trace(true)
7.  /* Wait for the session to complete the activity you want traced. */
8.  exec dbms_session.set_sql_trace(false)
```

Don't do that.[43]

These statements give you an Oracle version 6-style SQL trace (circa 1990), but not an *extended* SQL trace. You'll get only WAITS=>FALSE, BINDS=>FALSE output, which is almost never going to be what you want. When you don't trace syscalls ("waits"), you don't get enough information about how your time is being spent.

---

43. Except on ADB-S, where it's the only form of SQL tracing that you have access to (chapter 44).

44 Don't Trace with the DBMS_SYSTEM Package

Occasionally, we'll run across a DBA who still remembers the old DBMS_SYSTEM package. Don't trace with DBMS_SYSTEM. In fact, don't grant the EXECUTE privilege on DBMS_SYSTEM to anybody.

Every trace-related feature in DBMS_SYSTEM has a better alternative in either DBMS_MONITOR or DBMS_LOG.[44] Use those instead. Don't use DBMS_SYSTEM.

---

44. *Lewis, "dbms_log."*

45 Don't Trace with the DBMS_SUPPORT Package

The DBMS_SUPPORT package that was shipped with Oracle 9 was a godsend. It wasn't so much the function it performed—we could already do what we needed with DBMS_SYSTEM. The real value of DBMS_SUPPORT is that Oracle *supported* it, so Oracle customers no longer had to feel like tracing was dangerous or experimental. It officially opened Oracle tracing to the world.

With the advent of DBMS_MONITOR, released in Oracle Database 10g, there is no more need for DBMS_SUPPORT.

X   Autonomous Database

46 ADB Deployments

Oracle offers its Autonomous Database (ADB) in a choice of three deployments:

- Autonomous Database on *shared* infrastructure (ADB-S)
- Autonomous Database on *dedicated* infrastructure (ADB-D)
- Autonomous Database on *Cloud@Customer* infrastructure (C@C)

ADB-S and ADB-D are deployed on Oracle hardware, accessible through OCI. ADB C@C is deployed on hardware in your data center.

Oracle describes ADB-S as "like an autonomous vehicle with no need for a steering wheel or cruise control," and ADB-D as "like an autonomous vehicle that still includes a steering wheel and cruise control." ADB C@C is "Autonomous Database in your data center."[45]

Each implementation has its own tracing features and constraints. In general:

- ADB-S permits only Oracle 6-style (no-waits, no-binds) tracing, and it complicates trace file retrieval by prohibiting filesystem access.
- ADB-D is more permissive. It permits you to trace waits and binds for any session, but you may be denied access to the filesystem and some ALTER commands
- C@C is the most permissive ADB deployment. It gives you all the tracing features Oracle offers, and you get an OS prompt with root access.

---

45. Oracle, "FAQs for Autonomous Database."

47 Why Would You Ever Trace an ADB System?

When Oracle first released its self-driving Autonomous Database (ADB-S) in 2018, the product had *no* tracing feature. It was shocking: after three decades of releasing tracing features that made Oracle systems some of the most observable systems ever, Oracle's flagship database of the future was released with all forms of its tracing feature *disabled*. For people who traced, it was shocking.

But some people weren't shocked at all. They wondered why anyone would ever need to trace a program running on an automatically self-tuning database. The answer is, "Because observability is important, even in systems that are highly automated." For example:

- Without the feedback loop provided by tracing, how can software developers know whether the applications they're writing are correct and efficient? Poor interface design, poor data design, poor SQL, joins in the wrong tier, loops of dynamic SQL, row-by-row application logic—these are all problems that an autonomous database can't solve for you, and that are going to be much harder to find and fix if you can't trace anything.

- Even highly automated systems have defects. It's harder for everybody, including Oracle's own engineers, to work without a trace feature. Diagnosing and improving the ADB product itself is more difficult because its tracing feature is absent.

The people at Oracle know this. In 2021, after three years of trace enthusiasts despairing that ADB-S might *never* have a tracing feature, Oracle introduced the ability for an ADB-S session to control its own SQL_TRACE parameter. It's not a lot—this feature brought ADB-S tracing on par only with what Oracle version 6 could do in 1988—but it's a step in the right direction. We believe that future ADB-S releases will support more of the tracing features that Oracle has supported in the past.

48 Hello, World (ADB-D Remix)

Tracing on ADB-D is similar to tracing on non-ADB Oracle Database systems:

```
1. connect admin
2. exec dbms_monitor.session_trace_enable
3. select 'hello, world' from dual;
4. exec dbms_monitor.session_trace_disable
```

If you can't connect as ADMIN, then you'll need the following privilege granted to you by someone who can:

```
1. grant execute on dbms_monitor to dev1;
```

These statements will give you a WAITS=>TRUE, BINDS=>FALSE, PLAN_STAT=>'FIRST_EXECUTION' trace. You can control the tracing level with DBMS_MONITOR.

Some ADB-D implementations—for example, Exadata Cloud@Customer (ExaC@C)—give you filesystem access, so you can retrieve trace files just like you would on a conventional on-premises Oracle Database implementation. Other implementations may restrict your filesystem access, in which case you can query V$DIAG_TRACE_FILE_CONTENTS (chapter 14).

You may also find yourself subject to other restrictions on ADB-D. For example, you might be able to set STATISTICS_LEVEL but not MAX_DUMP_FILE_SIZE. You may or may not be able to create a DIRECTORY object for the directory named in V$DIAG_INFO. Understanding an ADB-D tracing feature's behavior requires testing.

49 Hello, World (ADB-S Remix)

Here's how you can create a "hello, world" trace on ADB-S:

```
1. connect admin
2. alter session set sql_trace=true;
3. select 'hello, world' from dual;
4. alter session set sql_trace=false;
5. select trace from session_cloud_trace order by row_number;
```

If you can't connect as ADMIN, then you'll need the following privileges granted to you by someone who can:

```
1. grant alter session to dev1;
2. grant read on session_cloud_trace to dev1;
```

Of course, the trace enablement method used here is a method we recommend against using (chapter 43), but unfortunately, a no-waits, no-binds trace is all you can get from ADB-S, at least for now.[46] You don't get access to DBMS_MONITOR, DBMS_SESSION.SESSION_TRACE_ENABLE, V$DIAG_TRACE_FILE_CONTENTS, or, of course, the filesystem. We don't know whether these constraints will be permanent.

---

46. See page xvii for Oracle Database versions that were current at this book's publication time.

50 Accessing ADB-S Traces

ADB-S doesn't provide filesystem access, which makes retrieving your traces more difficult. There are two ways to do it.

First, you can query SESSION_CLOUD_TRACE. This view contains a record of only *your* session's trace. When your session terminates, the content of SESSION_CLOUD_TRACE is gone. Its TRACE column (VARCHAR2(4000)) has a finite width, so if your SQL text is too long, Oracle can truncate it. We haven't found a way to work around this problem.[47]

Second, you can configure ADB-S to write traces to Oracle's Cloud Object Storage.[48] Your traces will be called:

bucket/sqltrace/*client*/*module*/sqltrace_*sid_serial*.trc

...where

- *bucket* is the value of the DEFAULT_LOGGING_BUCKET database property,

- *client* and *module* are your respective Oracle user session handle values, and

- *sid* and *serial* are your Oracle session ID and serial number. If you trace more than once in the same session, Oracle will append a unique _*n* to the *serial* value.

Unfortunately, the content in SESSION_CLOUD_TRACE and the Object Store are not identical. For example, a STAT line that is formatted as one line in the Object Store may be formatted as multiple lines in SESSION_CLOUD_TRACE.[49] It may not sound like a big deal, but the inconsistency makes it more difficult to write tools that read traces.

---

47. We can't solve it the way we did the V$DIAG_TRACE_FILE_CONTENTS problem (chapter 14), because ADB-S prohibits filesystem access through a database directory object.

48. *Oracle, "Perform SQL Tracing"; McDonald, "SQL trace."*

49. We were hoping that Oracle was formatting lines this way to avoid the 4,000-character SQL text length limit, but unfortunately, that's not the case—ADB doesn't format SQL text lines.

51 Does ADB Offer the Trace Features You Need?

ADB C@C is a full-featured platform where you can expect to have every tracing feature you'd expect on, say, a standard Oracle Enterprise Edition deployment.

ADB-D is a reasonably trace-friendly platform, although you might have a rough time retrieving the large numbers of trace files that would be created during an integration test or a troubleshooting project.

ADB-S, on the other hand, without even a WAITS=>TRUE trace facility, would be a frustrating platform to use for developing, testing, or troubleshooting any complex, high-performance application.

ADB is a young product whose tracing features are still evolving.[50] We recommend considering the considering observability scorecard as you evaluate which platform you'll use to develop, test, or run your next high-performance application:

1. Can you trace your own session (as with DBMS_MONITOR)?

2. Can you control MAX_DUMP_FILE_SIZE and STATISTICS_LEVEL?

3. Can you control WAITS, BINDS, and PLAN_STAT?

4. Can you access your own trace file content?

5. Can you trace a third-party session (as with DBMS_MONITOR)?

6. Can you access a third-party session's trace file content?

7. Can you trace a whole database (as with DBMS_MONITOR)?

8. Can you access thousands of trace files?[51]

9. Can you easily clean up unwanted trace files?

10. Can your application access all the trace-related packages it needs?

---

50. See page xvii for Oracle Database versions that were current at this book's publication time.

51. For people who have never seen a trace processor besides tkprof, it's hard to imagine why you might want more than one trace file at a time. But people with more sophisticated tools are accustomed to processing hundreds of traces at a time (chapter 52).

XI Method R Commercial Software

52 Method R Workbench

In the early 1990s, the only tool we had for summarizing Oracle trace data was Oracle's `tkprof`. That tool helped us get a lot of work done, but it ignored a lot of information in a trace file that we found important. In the early 2000s, we developed our own `tkprof` replacement called the Hotsos Profiler, which we wrote about in our 2003 book, *Optimizing Oracle Performance*. In 2008, we started a new company, and the Hotsos Profiler became known as the Method R Profiler.

Method R Profiler is special because it explains a program's duration in a receipt-like format that users, developers, and DBAs can all understand, like this:[52]

Contributor	Duration	Call count	Dur/call	
CPU	90	1,800	0.050	You might have envisioned a disk problem with this program because of its large disk I/O call count. But you'll never make this program noticeably faster without reducing its CPU consumption.
disk	6	6,000	0.001	
other	4	400	0.010	
Total	100	8,200	0.012	

Like `tkprof`, our profiler ate one `.trc` file at a time. In 2019, that changed in a big way. We built Method R Workbench[53] from the ground up to handle hundreds (and, today, thousands) of trace files at a time. All of the features from our beloved profiler are in there, but now, profiling is just a part of a much bigger story.

Method R Workbench helps you organize your traces. It makes simple work of identifying individual user experiences amid thousands of transactions traced within an application—even applications that use connection pooling. It can even generate data to create a Gantt chart in Excel that explains the flow of a complex network of batch processes. We work with Oracle traces all the time. We built Method R Workbench to be the tool we've always wanted.

---

52. Notice that in this table, the numbers in the *duration* column sum to the *total*. It may seem weird that we'd even mention that, but `tkprof` prints tables similar to this one where the numbers *don't* add up. That creates confusion and more work for the analyst.

53. *https://method-r.com/software/workbench*.

53 Method R Trace Extension for Oracle SQL Developer

Any time you trace a script in SQL Developer, you should do the following:

1. `alter session set max_dump_file_size=unlimited;`
2. `alter session set statistics_level=typical;`
3. `exec dbms_monitor.session_trace_enable`
4. *-- The code you want to trace goes here.*
5. `exec dbms_monitor.session_trace_disable`
6. `select value from v$diag_info where name='Default Trace File';`
7. *-- Go find your trace file and copy it to your desktop.*
8. *-- Discard any trace lines that aren't relevant to the most recent execution of your code.*

Lines 1, 2, 3, 5, and 6 are easy to understand but tiresome to type. Even if you write scripts to reduce the character count, bracketing your code every time you run it with `@trace-on` and `@trace-off` calls is tedious and error-prone.

Line 7 is more complicated. You know your trace file name from line 3, but how will you copy it from your database server (on which you may have no privileges) to your workstation?

Line 8 is even harder. A SQL Developer worksheet writes to just one trace file,[54] so all the traces executed within a given worksheet get concatenated into one big file. When you've retrieved that file, how will you identify the lines that correspond to just the one trace that you're interested in?

The Method R Trace extension for Oracle SQL Developer[55] does all this work for you. All eight steps, automatically, with no extra typing, and no extra clicks.

---

54. Except when you set TRACEFILE_IDENTIFIER (chapter 40) or use PX operations (chapter 30).

55. *https://method-r.com/software/trace.*

References

Amazon. "Oracle database log files." *Amazon Relational Database Service User Guide* (website), accessed September 14, 2022. *https://docs.aws.amazon.com/ AmazonRDS/latest/UserGuide/USER_LogAccess.Concepts.Oracle.html*.

Antognini, Christian. *Troubleshooting Oracle Performance*. New York, New York: Springer-Verlag, 2008.

Colgan, Maria. "What you can expect from Oracle Autonomous Transaction Processing." *SQL Maria* (blog), August 7, 2018. *https://sqlmaria.com/category/ autonomous-database/*.

Dontcheff, Julian. "SQL Trace and X-ADG in the Oracle Autonomous Database." *Julian Dontcheff's Database Blog* (blog), October 6, 2021. *https:// juliandontcheff.wordpress.com/2021/10/06/sql-trace-and-x-adg-in-the-oracle-autonomous-database/*.

Dontcheff, Julian. "Operating System access from within the Autonomous Database." *Julian Dontcheff's Database Blog* (blog), December 1, 2021. *https:// juliandontcheff.wordpress.com/2021/12/01/operating-system-access-from-within-the-autonomous-database/*.

Dyke, Julian, "Trace File Names." *juliandyke.com* (blog), accessed April 5, 2023. *http://www.juliandyke.com/Diagnostics/Trace/TraceFileNames.php*.

Holt, Jeff. "Fetching Oracle Trace Data from, Say, Amazon RDS." *Method R* (blog), December 31, 2021. *https://method-r.com/2021/12/31/oracle-trace-from-rds/*.

Kyte, Tom, "Slow by Slow…" *The Tom Kyte Blog* (blog), October 18, 2006. *https:// asktom.oracle.com/Misc/slow-by-slow.html*.

Lewis, Jonathan. "dbms_log." *Oracle Scratchpad* (blog), October 12, 2018. *https:// jonathanlewis.wordpress.com/2018/10/12/dbms_log/*.

Majors, Charity, Liz Fong-Jones, and George Miranda. *Observability Engineering: Achieving Production Excellence*. Sebastopol, California: O'Reilly, 2022.

McDonald, Connor. "SQL trace on your cloud database." *Connor McDonald* (blog), September 15, 2021. *https://connor-mcdonald.com/2021/09/15/sql-trace-on-your-cloud-database/*.

Millsap, Cary. "Oceans, Islands, and Rivers." *Method R* (blog), February 17, 2014. *https://method-r.com/2014/02/17/connection-pool-response-times-with-method-r-tools-oceans-islands-and-rivers/*.

Millsap, Cary, and Jeff Holt. *The Method R Guide to Mastering Oracle Trace Data.* Southlake, Texas: Method R, 2019. *https://method-r.com/motd*.

Millsap, Cary, with Jeff Holt. *Optimizing Oracle Performance: a Practitioner's Guide to Optimizing Response Time.* Sebastopol, California: O'Reilly, 2003.

Millsap, Cary. "I Can Help You Trace It." *Cary Millsap* (blog), November 18, 2011. *https://carymillsap.blogspot.com/2011/11/i-can-help-you-trace-it.html*.

Millsap, Cary. "Words I Don't Use, Part 5: 'Wait.'" *Cary Millsap* (blog), August 15, 2017. *https://carymillsap.blogspot.com/2017/08/words-i-dont-use-part-5-wait.html*.

Oracle Corporation. "Bug 31528203 : V$DIAG_TRACE_FILE_CONTENTS shows wrong line_number when payload > 4000 char." *My Oracle Support* (website), updated November 7, 2022. *https://support.oracle.com*.

Oracle Corporation. "FAQ: Common Tracing Techniques in Oracle E-Business Applications 11i and R12 (Doc ID 296559.1)." *My Oracle Support* (website), June 7, 2021. *https://support.oracle.com*.

Oracle Corporation. "FAQs for Autonomous Database." *Oracle Corporation* (website), accessed February 24, 2023. *https://www.oracle.com/database/technologies/datawarehouse-bigdata/adb-faqs.html*.

Oracle Corporation. "How to Collect 10046 Trace (SQL_TRACE) Diagnostics for Performance Issues (Doc ID 376442.1)." *My Oracle Support* (website), updated September 20, 2022. *https://support.oracle.com*.

Oracle Corporation. "How to Generate a SQLTrace Including Binds and Waits for a Concurrent Program in 11i and R12 (Doc ID 301372.1)." *My Oracle Support* (website), June 29, 2021. *https://support.oracle.com*.

Oracle Corporation. "Oracle E-Business SQL Trace and TKPROF Guide (Doc ID 1674024.1)." *My Oracle Support* (website), updated June 22, 2022. *https:// support.oracle.com.*

Oracle Corporation. "Performing Application Tracing." *Oracle Corporation* (website), accessed May 2, 2023. *https://docs.oracle.com/en/database/oracle/ oracle-database/19/tgsql/performing-application-tracing.html.*

Oracle Corporation. "Perform SQL Tracing on Autonomous Database." *Oracle Help Center* (website), accessed December 14, 2022. *https://docs.oracle.com/ en/cloud/paas/autonomous-database/adbsa/application-tracing.html.*

Oracle Corporation. "R12 11i: How to Obtain a Trace with Binds or Waits for Concurrent Processes in Oracle Projects (Doc ID 295963.1)." *My Oracle Support* (website), June 14, 2022. *https://support.oracle.com.*

Põder, Tanel. "ORADEBUG DOC." *tech.E2SN knowledge base* (website), accessed December 14, 2022. *http://tech.e2sn.com/oracle/troubleshooting/oradebug-doc.*

Põder, Tanel. "The Full Power of Oracle's Diagnostic Events, Part 2: ORADEBUG DOC and 11g Improvements." *Tanel Poder Consulting* (website), June 23, 2010. *https://tanelpoder.com/2010/06/23/the-full-power-of-oracles-diagnostic-events-part-2-oradebug-doc-and-11g-improvements/.*

Index

About the Authors

Cary Millsap spent the 1990s learning a lifetime's worth of lessons as a consultant at Oracle Corporation. He and the teams of performance specialists he recruited and trained at Oracle helped hundreds of customers around the world. In 1999, he left Oracle to co-found a company called Hotsos, which became renowned for its software, education, consulting, and annual performance-focused symposium event. In 2004, Cary and Jeff Holt were named *Oracle Magazine*'s Authors of the Year for creating *Optimizing Oracle Performance*, the first book ever to advocate using Oracle traces as a primary performance data source. In 2008, Cary founded Method R Corporation, which has served many of your favorite brands and created the world's first software system for managing, mining, and manipulating thousands of Oracle trace files. Cary is the author of *The Method R Guide to Mastering Oracle Trace Data* and *Faster: How to Optimize a System*. He has helped to educate thousands of information technology professionals through his commitment to writing and teaching. He is published in professional journals including *Communications of the ACM*.

Jeff Holt started his software optimization career in 1992 as a database administrator at AMR. In 1994, he joined Oracle Corporation as an onsite field support analyst for one of their Gold Support customers. In 1996, he joined Cary Millsap's elite System Performance Group, where he served seventeen more companies in multi-week engagements on four continents. In 1999, he became the founding chief scientist at Cary's new company called Hotsos Enterprises. In 2004, Cary and Jeff were named *Oracle Magazine*'s Authors of the Year for creating *Optimizing Oracle Performance*, the first book ever to advocate for using Oracle traces as a primary performance data source. In 2008, Jeff joined Cary at Method R Corporation where he is the lead developer, researcher, and support analyst for all of Method R's software products. He is a research contributor to *The Method R Guide to Mastering Oracle Trace Data*. Jeff is also an active consultant who helps customers around the world optimize and add features to their mission-critical systems.

Colophon

Cary Millsap designed the interior layouts and wrote the index using Adobe
InDesign. He used Mastermatic from Id-Extras to manage InDesign parent
page assignments. He designed the cover using Adobe Illustrator. The text font
is Minion Pro. Literals use Source Code Pro. Headings are Iowan Old Style. The
distinctive cover font is BorisBlackBloxx.

Other Books by the Authors

Making consistently great decisions about performance can be surprisingly easy, …*if* you understand what's going on. *Faster: How to Optimize a System* explains in a clear and thoughtful voice why systems perform the way they do. It is a book for anybody who is curious about how computer programs and other processes spend their time, and what you can do to improve them.

The *Method R Guide to Mastering Oracle Trace Data* is the definitive guide to accurate, high-precision measurement of user performance experiences, for Oracle application developers and DBAs. This book demonstrates how developers and DBAs can use Oracle trace data and Method R software to solve and prevent performance problems.

Optimizing Oracle Performance started an Oracle performance revolution. With this work, *Oracle Magazine*'s 2004 Authors of the Year defined not just the new response time optimization method called Method R, but the very standard by which performance improvement projects themselves should be measured.

www.ingramcontent.com/pod-product-compliance
Lightning Source LLC
La Vergne TN
LVHW051745050326
832903LV00029B/2726